Intro

The foundation of my life and ministry has come from what some have called "the secret place." It's that time that is set aside just for God. It's an uninterrupted time devoid of all other tasks, a space in our lives we carve out to be with Him.

The "secret place" is a time to be known and a time to discover the depth and beauty of the One who came to set us free from the bondage of sin and awaken us to His eternal purposes.

More than a professional explanation of who God is, we need a personal experience with God. The Psalmist tells us to "taste and see that the Lord is good" (Psalm 34:8).

This resource is to be used as a tool to help you gain an appetite for the goodness of God. It's been designed to help you experience His love, His grace, and His wisdom. Each day has been laid out in such a way that you interact with the scripture, note your observations, determine how this truth applies to your life, and commit those things to prayer. There is intentional space for you to record whatever God is speaking and however the spirit is leading you.

As you use this scripture journal my hope and my prayer is that you experience God T O D A Y in a personal way. In a way that you would be transformed from the inside out. In a way that the life you live, and the world you engage with will never be the same.

Aaron DeLoach

Scriptures are from the New Living Translation version unless otherwise noted.

DAY 1

³All praise to God, the Father of our Lord Jesus Christ. God is our merciful Father and the source of all comfort. ⁴He comforts us in all our troubles so that we can comfort others. When they are troubled, we will be able to give them the same comfort God has given us.

2 Corinthians 1:3-4

DAY 2

For I command you this day to love the Lord your God and to keep his commands, decrees, and regulations by walking in his ways. If you do this, you will live and multiply, and the Lord your God will bless you and the land you are about to enter and occupy.

Deuteronomy 30:16

DAY 3

If you need wisdom, ask our generous God, and he will give it to you. He will not rebuke you for asking.

James 1:5

EXTRA TIME →

Just ASK!

Where there is NEED in our lives, God has provided a way... Just ASK!

How could it be that simple?!? Well, He is a generous God. It is who He is. He can't help but to be generous. God always acts in ways that are consistent to His character.

When we ASK our Heavenly Father he will not rebuke us like an earthly father might. He won't send us away saying, "Why do you need that? Why did you ask for that? Are you serious? You can't figure that out on your own?"

No! He loves that we come to Him in our NEED. He wants us to seek His wisdom because His ways and thoughts are higher and better than ours (Is. 55:8). His ways bring blessings to our lives and are for our benefit. Our Heavenly Father wants what is best for His kids.

It is truly best when our hearts and minds become more like His. We then begin to make decisions the way He would and start thinking like He does. We start to ask questions like, "Jesus, if you were me right now, what would you choose to do?"

↗

Begin to ask Him right now to meet you at that point of need.

*If you get a chance, read James 1:1-5 and notice that verse 5 is the answer to the troubles that come in verse 2. Verses 3 & 4 are the encouragement while you are in the trouble and waiting for the answer.

What areas of your life do you need wisdom?

What practices can you adopt to help you remember to ASK more often (set an alarm, put a note on your mirror, etc.)?

¹¹Furthermore, because we are united with Christ, we have received an inheritance from God, for he chose us in advance, and he makes everything work out according to his plan. ¹²God's purpose was that we Jews who were the first to trust in Christ would bring praise and glory to God.

Ephesians 1:11-12

DAY 5

¹⁰When the people saw the cloud standing at the entrance of the tent, they would stand and bow down in front of their own tents. Inside the Tent of Meeting, the Lord would speak to Moses face to face, as one speaks to a friend. Afterward Moses would return to the camp, but the young man who assisted him, Joshua son of Nun, would remain behind in the Tent of Meeting.

Exodus 33:10-11

EXTRA TIME

Israelites **SAW** God.
Moses **SPOKE** to God.
Joshua **STAYED** with God.

His presence prepares you for His purpose. God had a purpose for Joshua's life that he couldn't see coming...

¹After the death of Moses the servant of the Lord, the Lord said to Joshua the son of Nun, Moses' assistant, ²"Moses my servant is dead. Now therefore arise, go over this Jordan, you and all this people, into the land that I am giving to them, to the people of Israel. ³Every place that the sole of your foot will tread upon I have given to you, just as I promised to Moses."

Joshua 1:1-3

Like Joshua, God has a purpose for your life. As you step out to lead there is no more important task than to stay in His presence. This is your greatest ministry assignment: STAY

DAY 6

"[28]I give them eternal life, and they will never perish. No one can snatch them away from me, [29]for my Father has given them to me, and he is more powerful than anyone else. No one can snatch them from the Father's hand. [30]The Father and I are one."

John 10:28-30

The temptations in your life are no different from what others experience. And God is faithful. He will not allow the temptation to be more than you can stand. When you are tempted, he will show you a way out so that you can endure.

1 Corinthians 10:1

DAY 8

⁹So let's not get tired of doing what is good. At just the right time we will reap a harvest of blessing if we don't give up. ¹⁰Therefore, whenever we have the opportunity, we should do good to everyone—especially to those in the family of faith.

Galatians 6:9-10

EXTRA TIME

Especially

In the scripture today the word ESPECIALLY stands out to me. I have always thought I was supposed to do good to everyone, but especially to the unbeliever. Like, I was supposed to start with the lost and be a witness of the goodness of God.

Seemed logical to me. However, it is very clear that I was wrong! That is NOT what these verses say! In the original Greek language the word especially is the word málista. It means especially, chiefly, most of all, above all.

It's a reminder that the good that God has called us to do should begin with the believer first and THEN flow to the unbeliever. As you consider your local family of faith, what names come to mind that God is asking you to do good for today? This week? Or even this month?

↗

Maybe God will give you more insight as you read Galatians 6:9-10 in The Message paraphrase:

Galatians 6:9-10 (MSG) So let's not allow ourselves to get fatigued doing good. At the right time we will harvest a good crop if we don't give up, or quit. Right now, therefore, every time we get the chance, let us work for the benefit of all, starting with the people closest to us in the community of faith.

Write a couple things you will do for the names of the believers God brought to your mind.

DAY 8

[20] Now all glory to God, who is able, through his mighty power at work within us, to accomplish infinitely more than we might ask or think. [21] Glory to him in the church and in Christ Jesus through all generations forever and ever! Amen.

Ephesians 3:20-21

DAY 9

I appeal to you, dear brothers and sisters, by the authority of our Lord Jesus Christ, to live in harmony with each other. Let there be no divisions in the church. Rather, be of one mind, united in thought and purpose.

1 Corinthians 1:10

DAY 10

¹Therefore I, a prisoner for serving the Lord, beg you to lead a life worthy of your calling, for you have been called by God. ²Always be humble and gentle. Be patient with each other, making allowance for each other's faults because of your love. ³Make every effort to keep yourselves united in the Spirit, binding yourselves together with peace.

Ephesians 4:1-3

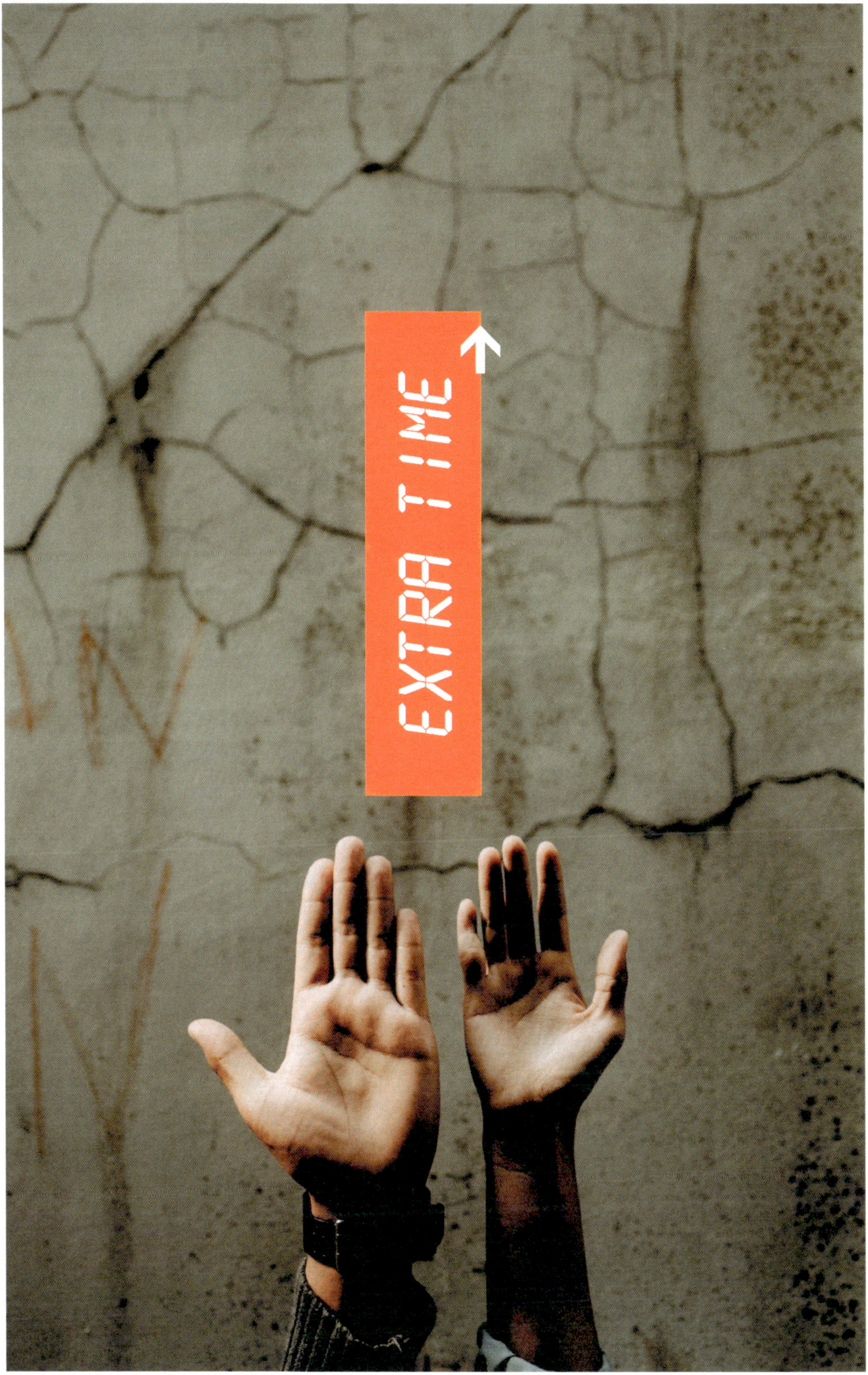
EXTRA TIME

Unity Builders

I was leading a group of professional soccer players into a Congolese village on a mission trip and had delegated some tasks to our team as we prepared for departure. After a hot and bumpy 8-hour bus ride, we arrived to set up our camp. I quickly realized, while we were unloading that the most important task hadn't been completed.

Clean drinking water failed to make it onto our bus, and I was frustrated. The team could see it on my face and hear it in my voice as I called out the player who was responsible for the water in front of the entire team.

The words of my mouth and the attitudes of my heart were divisive, as I was wanting everyone to know that it was not my fault. In that moment, I was not living a life worthy of my calling.

Calling is a word that creates confusion in the Christian community, but it doesn't have to. We are all called to make every effort to stay unified in the Spirit. Humility, gentleness, and patience are unity builders. As we operate from these attitudes we make allowances for the faults of other believers, including a silly thing like water.

Unity is more important than you might think. Jesus reminded us that the watching world would know we are his disciples by our love for one another (John 13:35).

How much effort have you been giving to maintaining unity with other believers?

If humility, gentleness, & patience build unity, what types of attitudes destroy unity?

Why is maintaining unity a worthy calling?

How will you unify believers today? Who do you need to call? What do you need to say or not say?

DAY 11

¹Oh, the joys of those who do not follow the advice of the wicked, or stand around with sinners, or join in with mockers. ²But they delight in the law of the Lord, meditating on it day and night.

Psalm 1:1-2

DAY 12

⁵May God, who gives this patience and encouragement, help you live in complete harmony with each other, as is fitting for followers of Christ Jesus. ⁶Then all of you can join together with one voice, giving praise and glory to God, the Father of our Lord Jesus Christ.

Romans 15:5-6

DAY 13

"[20]All who do evil hate the light and refuse to go near it for fear their sins will be exposed. [21]But those who do what is right come to the light so others can see that they are doing what God wants."

John 3:20-21

EXTRA TIME →

Say Yes

Has the power ever gone out in your house and you found yourself with a flashlight in hand?

Isn't it amazing how even the smallest light can be visible in the midst of ALL the darkness? The Bible tells us that Jesus is the light of the world, but people have chosen to stay in the shadows even though they have the option to walk into the light and discover purpose, destiny, and direction for their life.

Out of FEAR they wander in the darkness trying to find what they are looking for. FEAR is one of the enemy's greatest tricks. Fear keeps you and me in our sin because we are afraid of what others might think of us.

And here is the trick for us: if we can remember that what God thinks of us is more important than what others think of us, we can find FREEDOM! We can walk into the light knowing that God has our best interests in mind and wants to see us made healthy and whole again.

Those who do what is right find it easier to repent when they do wrong. Every time we say YES to God and NO to sin it gets easier to step into the light. In this way, we expose the greatness of our God, who loves each of us regardless of our past mistakes and failures.

I am so grateful that my past mistakes and failures don't disqualify me from God's love. The truth is, no matter who you are or what you have done in the "darkness" you are still welcome in the family of God.

What areas of your life have you been hiding in the dark? Ask the Holy Spirit to show you now.

What fears have held you back from being free?

Take some time to come into the light and repent to God anything you have been hiding. Ask for His strength to say YES to His ways and NO to sin. After all... he already knows you better than you know yourself.

DAY 14

¹⁷But the wisdom from above is first of all pure. It is also peace loving, gentle at all times, and willing to yield to others. It is full of mercy and the fruit of good deeds. It shows no favoritism and is always sincere. ¹⁸And those who are peacemakers will plant seeds of peace and reap a harvest of righteousness.

James 3:17-18

DAY 15

And the Lord said, "That's right, and it means that I am watching, and I will certainly carry out all my plans."

Jeremiah 1:12

DAY 16

But we are citizens of heaven, where the Lord Jesus Christ lives. And we are eagerly waiting for him to return as our Savior.

Philippians 3:20

DAY 17

And now, dear brothers and sisters, one final thing. Fix your thoughts on what is true, and honorable, and right, and pure, and lovely, and admirable. Think about things that are excellent and worthy of praise.

Philippians 4:8

⁶So letting your sinful nature control your mind leads to death. But letting the Spirit control your mind leads to life and peace. ⁷For the sinful nature is always hostile to God. It never did obey God's laws, and it never will. ⁸That's why those who are still under the control of their sinful nature can never please God.

Romans 8:6-8

EXTRA TIME →

Taking Time

A few years ago I got my son a remote-control car. Immediately he fell in love. He was driving it inside, outside, & everywhere in between. He loved how the car responded to the directional control in his hand.

One day the car started to malfunction. He would tell the car to go forward and it would reverse; he would tell it to go left and it would go right. The car was no longer responding to the remote control. The wires had gotten crossed and the machine wasn't thinking properly.

The car ended up crashing itself into the wall and was no longer useful. If we aren't careful, this can happen to us spiritually. As believers, we have the spirit of God living in us. We are called to let him lead and be in control. With every NUDGE of the spirit we are to respond.

When he is in control, we move forward or backwards, right or left, only as he prompts. Our decision making, thinking, and actions are in response to the Spirit at work in us. The Spirit of God will always lead you to act in accordance with the Word of God. When you do, it brings life and peace to you and all those around you.

But too often, we follow our sinful nature rather than our spirit nature. We bulldoze through the commands of scripture and the promptings of the spirit out of our selfishness.

When we are absorbed in ourselves, we ignore God.

In The Message paraphrase of the Bible, Romans 8:7 says, "That person ignores God and what he is doing." This type of thinking not only brings spiritual death, but death to our relationships.

What areas or decisions have you bulldozed through the Spirit's promptings?

If you followed the Spirit's prompting today, who would you encourage? Who would you take to lunch? To whom would you take time to listen?

Talk to God right now, and ask Him to help you respond to Him today. Pray for your interactions with the people you named above.

DAY 19

Commit everything you do to the Lord.
Trust him, and he will help you.

Psalm 37:5

DAY 20

Love each other with genuine affection, and take delight in honoring each other.

Romans 12:10

DAY 21

But we are citizens of heaven, where the Lord Jesus Christ lives. And we are eagerly waiting for him to return as our Savior.

Philippians 3:20

DAY 22

And now, dear brothers and sisters, one final thing. Fix your thoughts on what is true, and honorable, and right, and pure, and lovely, and admirable. Think about things that are excellent and worthy of praise.

Philippians 4:8

EXTRA TIME →

Philippians 4:8-9 The Message (MSG)
"Summing it all up, friends, I'd say you'll do best by filling your minds and meditating on things true, noble, reputable, authentic, compelling, gracious—the best, not the worst; the beautiful, not the ugly; things to praise, not things to curse."

Your mind is powerful, and has a way of dictating your behavior. That is one of the reasons the Apostle Paul commands believers in Romans 12:2 to be transformed by the renewing of your mind.

You are at your best when you are thinking on things that are true, honorable, right, pure, lovely, and admirable.

List one thing in each category to which you can fix your mind.

True:

Honorable:

Right:

Pure:

Lovely:

Admirable:

When you think on these things, there won't be any room in your mind for you to think on destructive things.

DAY 23

¹³For "Everyone who calls on the name of the Lord will be saved." ¹⁴But how can they call on him to save them unless they believe in him? And how can they believe in him if they have never heard about him? And how can they hear about him unless someone tells them?

Romans 10:13-14

DAY 24

[1]I waited patiently for the Lord to help me, and he turned to me and heard my cry. [2]He lifted me out of the pit of despair, out of the mud and the mire. He set my feet on solid ground and steadied me as I walked along.

Psalm 40:1-2

DAY 25

Love each other with genuine affection, and take delight in honoring each other.

Romans 12:10

DAY 26

God's law was given so that all people could see how sinful they were. But as people sinned more and more, God's wonderful grace became more abundant.

Romans 5:20

EXTRA TIME ↓

I love to eat

I love to eat. American food, Chinese food, Ethiopian food, Mexican food, you name it and I will eat it.

Sometimes I leave a meal needing a little something extra, but I don't exactly know what I need until it is presented as an option. My pantry may have something salty like chips, but that doesn't sound right. My fridge might have something fruity like an orange, but that doesn't sound right either. After one or two more options, I find the exact right mix of flavors and textures to fulfill my need.

But here is the thing, I could never have told you what I needed prior to it being presented.

God's law was given so we could know what we need. The law shows us how sinful we are, and the need we have for a savior. The more we are aware of our sin, the more aware we are of God's grace that is poured out on us in abundance.

This is the joy we have as believers. We are sinners saved by grace. We are deserving of nothing, but God has given us everything through Jesus Christ.

The Old Testament law was never given so we could keep it perfectly. It was given so we could see that we could never keep it perfectly. The law was given to establish Jesus as the only means of achieving right standing with God.

In what ways is this truth about the law enlightening?

How should understanding the depth of our need for a savior change the way we live?

Pray and ask God to show you the depths of your sin and the abundance of his grace.

What one person in your life needs to know why the law was given? Record their name and what you will say below. Contact them today.

DAY 27

So let's not get tired of doing what is good. At just the right time we will reap a harvest of blessing if we don't give up.

Galatians 6:9

And I am certain that God, who began the good work within you, will continue his work until it is finally finished on the day when Christ Jesus returns.

Philippians 1:6

DAY 29

"And you will recognize him by this sign: You will find a baby wrapped snugly in strips of cloth, lying in a manger."

Luke 2:12

DAY 30

So we don't look at the troubles we can see now; rather, we fix our gaze on things that cannot be seen. For the things we see now will soon be gone, but the things we cannot see will last forever.

2 Corinthians 4:18

DAY 31

Bring all the tithes into the storehouse so there will be enough food in my Temple. If you do," says the Lord of Heaven's Armies, "I will open the windows of heaven for you. I will pour out a blessing so great you won't have enough room to take it in! Try it! Put me to the test!"

Malachi 3:10

EXTRA TIME →

He is Faithful

Several years ago a friend and I were sitting at his kitchen table. Our kids were playing together in the backyard and our wives were talking in the living room. At the table we began a conversation about giving and this question was posed: "How much is too much?"

We concluded on that day that we could never be too generous in giving what God had given to us. After further thought I realized that I would never get to heaven and regret giving. However, it could be true that I would get to heaven and regret NOT giving.

I will never stand before God and say, "I wish I wouldn't have given so much."

The theme of generosity is weaved throughout the Scriptures. We see the tithe (a tenth of all of our increase) given to the Lord before anything else. In this way we acknowledge that God is the giver of all things. What I have seen in my life is that the 90% that I have left seems to always go further than the 100% I would have have kept.

In the New Testament we see the believers giving far beyond the tithe. We see they gave sacrificially, they gave cheerfully, and they gave regularly. As we give of the finances God has placed in our hands according to the Biblical pattern, we are being obedient.

The blessings of obedience can't always be seen, measured, or counted, but God promises he will bless and provide for us. If there is one thing I have learned, it is that we can trust God... HE IS FAITHFUL.

How do you feel when people talk about God and money in the same sentence? Why?

What keeps you from generosity?

Most of us don't give sacrificially (when was the last time you did?), few of us do so cheerfully, and many of us are likely more sporadic than regular in our giving. Pray and ask God to help you become a sacrificial, cheerful, and regular giver.

DAY 32

So you have not received a spirit that makes you fearful slaves. Instead, you received God's Spirit when he adopted you as his own children. Now we call him, "Abba, Father."

Romans 8:15

DAY 33

¹Out of the stump of David's family will grow a shoot—yes, a new Branch bearing fruit from the old root. ²And the Spirit of the Lord will rest on him— the Spirit of wisdom and understanding, the Spirit of counsel and might, the Spirit of knowledge and the fear of the Lord.

Isaiah 11:1-2

DAY 34

Jesus replied, "All who love me will do what I say. My Father will love them, and we will come and make our home with each of them."

John 14:23

DAY 35

"Father, if you are willing, please take this cup of suffering away from me. Yet I want your will to be done, not mine."

Luke 22:42

DAY 36

¹In the beginning God created the heavens and the earth. ²The earth was formless and empty, and darkness covered the deep waters. And the Spirit of God was hovering over the surface of the waters.

Genesis 1:1-2

EXTRA TIME

> [1] In the beginning God created the heavens and the earth. [2] The earth was formless and empty, and darkness covered the deep waters. And the Spirit of God was hovering over the surface of the waters.
>
> Genesis 1:1-2

My observations

God was pre-existent before anything.

God can create something out of nothing.

God is good.

God is always active in the world & in your life.

What type of impact can these four truths have on your daily life?

DAY 37

For just as the Father gives life to those he raises from the dead, so the Son gives life to anyone he wants.

John 5:21

DAY 38

²"This is what the Lord says—the Lord who made the earth, who formed and established it, whose name is the Lord: ³Ask me and I will tell you remarkable secrets you do not know about things to come."

Jeremiah 33:2-3

DAY 39

But the Lord said to Samuel, "Don't judge by his appearance or height, for I have rejected him. The Lord doesn't see things the way you see them. People judge by outward appearance, but the Lord looks at the heart."

1 Samuel 16:7

DAY 40

But we are citizens of heaven, where the Lord Jesus Christ lives. And we are eagerly waiting for him to return as our Savior.

Philippians 3:20

DAY 41

Don't love money; be satisfied with what you have. For God has said, "I will never fail you. I will never abandon you."

Hebrews 13:5

EXTRA TIME

This & That

I'm easily distracted, not ADD, but close. My mind moves a million miles per hour in a million different directions. "Can you relate?"

With so much movement, it is easy to be distracted.

As believers, we are easily distracted from God, who is supposed to be our one central focus. The enemy of our soul will use just about anything to get us off track, including the love of money. The problem isn't when we have money, the problem is when money has us.

We all tend to want more money; money breeds security and in a lot of cases "satisfaction." In this passage, we are instructed to be fully satisfied in what we have because God is the one who will provide security. He won't fail us. He won't let us down or leave us. He has all we need, and in Him we are complete.

Notice the passage doesn't say DON'T HAVE MONEY or DON'T USE MONEY, it says DON'T LOVE MONEY. Why? What's the difference?

How can money be distracting?

In learning to deal with money, why does it matter that God won't fail us, let us down, or leave us?

DAY 42

Are any of you suffering hardships? You should pray. Are any of you happy? You should sing praises.

James 5:13

DAY 43

We can make our plans, but
the Lord determines our steps.

Proverbs 16:9

DAY 44

[3] With joy you will drink deeply from the fountain of salvation! [4] In that wonderful day you will sing: "Thank the Lord! Praise his name! Tell the nations what he has done. Let them know how mighty he is!

Isaiah 12:3-4

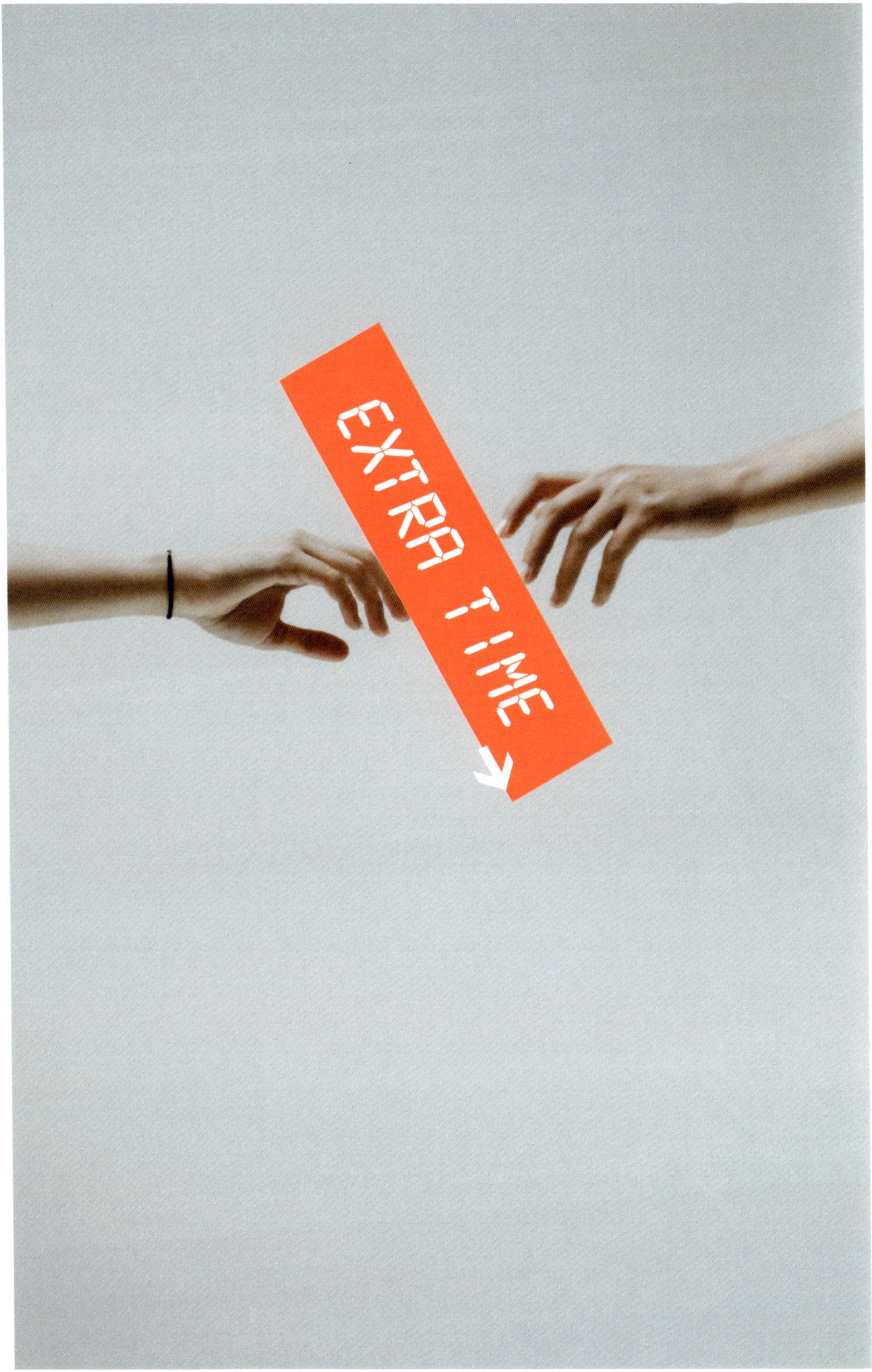
EXTRA TIME

Let's Face It

You've seen it before. I've seen it before. Let's face it... we have all seen it.

It's that epic battle scene where an unforeseen hero steps up from the underdog army and single handedly brings victory to their people. Salvation has come, shouts of joy and songs of praise can be heard in the surrounding nations. These shouts and songs bring praise to the Hero who has won the victory and soon his name is made famous throughout the Earth. People begin telling stories of what their mighty Hero has done for generations to come.

Like I said... we have all seen this before, but this is not a new story line.

The Lord Jesus Christ was and is this Hero for the people of God. In the Old Testament we see God saving the people of Israel bringing salvation from their enemies. Often times there was dancing, singing, and shouting praises to God!

May we never stop singing and sharing about the joy of our salvation. May we never stop talking about the ONE who has saved us and won the victory. May we not stop telling each other of all he continues to do in our lives. As we do, our faith builds, and our confidence in the creator increases. As you engage in conversation today with others, ask these questions "What is God teaching you lately? How has he been speaking to you? What mighty things is he doing in your life?"

When you do, his fame will spread around the globe for generations to come!

What difference does it make to know that Jesus is the Hero who single handedly won the victory for your salvation?

When you are feeling defeated how do you remind yourself of the JOY of your salvation?

Is your natural tendency to rejoice and thank the Lord? If not, why is this so hard to do?

Who is God asking you to engage in conversation today? Talk about what He has been speaking to you and the mighty things He is doing in your life.

DAY 45

"Do not judge others, and you will not be judged."

Matthew 7:1

DAY 46

"Look! I stand at the door and knock. If you hear my voice and open the door, I will come in, and we will share a meal together as friends."

Revelation 3:20

DAY 47

If you think you are too important to help someone, you are only fooling yourself. You are not that important.

Galatians 6:3

DAY 48

Some nations boast of their chariots and horses, but we boast in the name of the Lord our God.

Psalm 20:7

Journal

Take a few minutes to pour your heart out to God. Write what's on your mind, what's bothering you, ask him questions, and record what he has been speaking to you. Whatever it is, this space is for you.

⁵Trust in the Lord with all your heart; do not depend on your own understanding. ⁶Seek his will in all you do, and he will show you which path to take.

Proverbs 3:5-6

DAY 50

And we know that the Son of God has come, and he has given us understanding so that we can know the true God. And now we live in fellowship with the true God because we live in fellowship with his Son, Jesus Christ. He is the only true God, and he is eternal life.

1 John 5:20

EXTRA TIME →

Dive Deeper

Colossians says it like this, "He (Jesus) is the visible image of the invisible God." In other words, when we examine Jesus' life and teaching, it reveals who this invisible God is and how He operates. Have you ever examined the life of Jesus? If you want to know what God is like you should examine the life of Jesus in the Gospels and in historical writings from non-Christian historians like Flavius Josephus.

Jesus is not some fairy tale character. He really walked the face of this Earth. Jesus is not one way among many ways to know the true God. He is the only way (John 14:6). As we trust in the work He came to do, we receive eternal life. It starts the moment we trust Him, not the moment we die (John 17:3). Death does not get the last word in our lives!

[55]"Where, O death, is your victory? Where, O death, is your sting?" [56]The sting of death is sin, and the power of sin is the law. [57]But thanks be to God! He gives us the victory through our Lord Jesus Christ. [58]Therefore, my dear brothers and sisters, stand firm. Let nothing move you. Always give yourselves fully to the work of the Lord, because you know that your labor in the Lord is not in vain.

1 Corinthians 15:55-58

What do the scriptures teach about salvation, eternal life, and the way to the Father in heaven?

According to research, 45% of Americans say there are many ways to heaven. What are the ways that you have heard?

Take some extra time right now to pray that the world would come to see Jesus as the way, the truth, and the life.

DAY 51

And whatever you do or say, do it as a representative of the Lord Jesus, giving thanks through him to God the Father.

Colossians 3:17

DAY 52

Pray in the Spirit at all times and on every occasion. Stay alert and be persistent in your prayers for all believers everywhere.

Ephesians 6:18

DAY 53

For the Kingdom of God is not just a lot of talk; it is living by God's power.

1 Corinthians 4:20

DAY 54

From one man Adam, he created all the nations throughout the whole earth. He decided beforehand when they should rise and fall, and he determined their boundaries.

Acts 17:26

DAY 55

The members of the council were amazed when they saw the boldness of Peter and John, for they could see that they were ordinary men with no special training in the Scriptures. They also recognized them as men who had been with Jesus

Acts 4:13

DAY 56

"For the Lord your God is living among you. He is a mighty savior. He will take delight in you with gladness. With his love, he will calm all your fears. He will rejoice over you with joyful songs."

Zephaniah 3:17

Journal

Take a few minutes to pour your heart out to God. Write what's on your mind, what's bothering you, ask him questions, and record what he has been speaking to you. Whatever it is, this space is for you.

DAY 57

The Lord is merciful and compassionate, slow to get angry and filled with unfailing love.

Psalm 145:8

DAY 58

But let all who take refuge in you rejoice; let them sing joyful praises forever. Spread your protection over them, that all who love your name may be filled with joy.

Psalm 5:11

EXTRA TIME →

Great Joy

When you were a kid did you ever play a game that was safe and protected like "Hide and Seek"?

I loved the thrill of hiding and trying to outrun the seeker to safety. It was in that place of refugee that my face would light up and I would rejoice as I waited for the others to arrive safely. One by one they would arrive and with great excitement. We would talk about our amazing hiding places and the great spin move or juke we used to get to the base. We would go on and on so full of joy.

When we lean into God as our refuge, our place of safety, we should be filled with great joy. He provided a way for us to escape the death we deserved. In Him, we are protected from the evil one. The Bible makes it clear that "greater is he that is in me than he that is in the world" (1 John 4:4). This passage gives us great confidence in our God who is stronger than the evil we face.

Our joy in this truth should overwhelm us and result in singing praises to his name. Not that you have to be the most musical person on the planet...believe me, I'm not. But luckily, God cares more about your heart than the noise he hears! My prayer is that you would be undone by his greatness, that you would speak of the great things he has done, and as a result, the people of God would be the most joyful people on the planet!

"Have you ever read 1 John? It's short and one of my favorites. Most of the New Testament books are actually letters, and are originally intended to be read in one sitting. Grab your Bible and give it a try!"

Have you taken refuge in God, or tried to find security and safety in yourself?

What do you have to rejoice about? How can you sing his praises today?

What do you think is the difference between happiness and joy?

Take some time to pray that your security in this life wouldn't be derived from money, power, status, possessions, or performance. Pray that it would come from the truth that our great God is yours, and you are His.

DAY 59

Don't be selfish; don't try to impress others. Be humble, thinking of others as better than yourselves.

Philippians 2:3

DAY 60

"That is why I tell you not to worry about everyday life—whether you have enough food and drink, or enough clothes to wear. Isn't life more than food, and your body more than clothing?"

Matthew 6:25

DAY 61

I will never forget your commandments,
for by them you give me life.

Psalm 119:93

DAY 62

The next day John saw Jesus coming toward him and said, "Look! The Lamb of God who takes away the sin of the world!"

John 1:29

EXTRA TIME →

Throughout the Scriptures Jesus is given many different names. They speak to His various attributes and what he came to do. The Lamb of God, here in John 1, is highly significant. Think back through the Old Testament and anything you might know of the sacrificial system used to cover the sins of the people of Israel. The people were instructed to sacrifice a spotless lamb without blemish. When John points out Jesus as the Lamb of God who takes away the sins of the world, he is alluding to Jesus coming to live a perfectly sinless life, and paying the penalty for our sin by dying in our place on the cross. Jesus' sacrifice didn't just cover sin temporarily, it erased sin permanently.

Take some time to look up the following verses. Next to each passage list the name(s) given to Jesus. Below the verses indicate which name you like the most and why.

Isaiah 7:14
He is...

Isaiah 9:6
He is...

Peter 5:4
He is...

1 Timothy 6:15
He is...

DAY 63

Hypocrite! First get rid of the log in your own eye; then you will see well enough to deal with the speck in your friend's eye.

Matthew 7:5

DAY 64

For the Lord will pass through the land to strike down the Egyptians. But when he sees the blood on the top and sides of the doorframe, the Lord will pass over your home. He will not permit his death angel to enter your house and strike you down.

Exodus 12:23

DAY 65

⁶Don't worry about anything; instead, pray about everything. Tell God what you need, and thank him for all he has done. ⁷Then you will experience God's peace, which exceeds anything we can understand. His peace will guard your hearts and minds as you live in Christ Jesus.

Philippians 4:6-7

EXTRA TIME →

His Peace

Don't worry seems like a pretty tall order. I run into people everywhere I go who are worried. Every one of us worries. We have places to go, and people to see. We have work that needs to get done, kids that need to be picked up, money that needs to be made, food to be cooked, laundry to keep up with, and commitments that need to be honored.

Let's face it, we run a pretty hectic schedule. Worry is not something we can get rid of easily. But what would happen if every time worry creeped into your mind you immediately prayed about it? What if your to do list for the day became your prayer list for the day? What if you began to tell God what you needed, and thanked him for all the things he has already done?

When we rely on His power and remember His promises, we experience His peace.

When I remember God's faithfulness, I can take a few deep breaths and trust the bumps in my schedule have not surprised God. If He took care of me before, then he will take care of me again. Just a quick side note, he is powerful enough to handle anything that may come.

Could it be that we feel worried because we are taking on more responsibilities that we were ever meant to carry? Perhaps God's peace stands as a guard over our hearts and minds to keep wrong thinking out. When I think God's job is my job, I get overwhelmed.

Write your "To Do List" today and then take time to pray through it. Make it your prayer list and keep your eyes open for the PRINCE OF PEACE... He is coming!

[DAY 66]

⁷"When you pray, don't babble on and on as the Gentiles do. They think their prayers are answered merely by repeating their words again and again. ⁸Don't be like them, for your Father knows exactly what you need even before you ask him!

Matthew 6:7-8

DAY 67

And it is impossible to please God without faith. Anyone who wants to come to him must believe that God exists and that he rewards those who sincerely seek him.

Hebrews 11:6

DAY 68

God blesses those who patiently endure testing and temptation. Afterward they will receive the crown of life that God has promised to those who love him.

James 1:12

Journal

Take a few minutes to pour your heart out to God. Write what's on your mind, what's bothering you, ask him questions, and record what he has been speaking to you. Whatever it is, this space is for you.

DAY 69

You didn't choose me. I chose you. I appointed you to go and produce lasting fruit, so that the Father will give you whatever you ask for, using my name.

John 15:16

Understand, therefore, that the Lord your God is indeed God. He is the faithful God who keeps his covenant for a thousand generations and lavishes his unfailing love on those who love him and obey his commands.

Deuteronomy 7:9

DAY 71

Dear friends, you always followed my instructions when I was with you. And now that I am away, it is even more important. Work hard to show the results of your salvation, obeying God with deep reverence and fear.

Philippians 2:12

Preach the word of God. Be prepared, whether the time is favorable or not. Patiently correct, rebuke, and encourage your people with good teaching.

2 Timothy 4:2

EXTRA TIME →

Use your pen and note the differences in translation. How do they enhance your understanding of why we are to preach the word? Circle things that stand out to you. Make notes and record your questions in the margins.

(Share what God speaks with you today on social media using the hashtag #todayscripturejournal and @todayscripturejournal)

Preach the word; be prepared in season and out of season; correct, rebuke and encourage—with great patience and careful instruction.

2 Timothy 4:2 (NIV)

Preach the word [as an official messenger]; be ready when the time is right and even when it is not [keep your sense of urgency, whether the opportunity seems favorable or unfavorable, whether convenient or inconvenient, whether welcome or unwelcome]; correct [those who err in doctrine or behavior], warn [those who sin], exhort and encourage [those who are growing toward spiritual maturity], with inexhaustible patience and [faithful] teaching.

2 Timothy 4:2 (AMP)

I can't impress this on you too strongly. God is looking over your shoulder. Christ himself is the Judge, with the final say on everyone, living and dead. He is about to break into the open with his rule, so proclaim the Message with intensity; keep on your watch. Challenge, warn, and urge your people. Don't ever quit. Just keep it simple.

2 Timothy 4:1-2 (MSG)

DAY 73

For God is working in you, giving you the desire and the power to do what pleases him.

Philippians 2:13

DAY 74

"Those who accept my commandments and obey them are the ones who love me. And because they love me, my Father will love them. And I will love them and reveal myself to each of them."

John 14:21

²⁹"And don't be concerned about what to eat and what to drink. Don't worry about such things. ³⁰These things dominate the thoughts of unbelievers all over the world, but your Father already knows your needs. ³¹Seek the Kingdom of God above all else, and he will give you everything you need."

Luke 29-31

EXTRA TIME →

Unseen Kingdom

There is more to life than what we see. If you have ever studied an iceberg then you know this is true. Scientists will tell you that what we see is roughly 10% of the iceberg, leaving 90% left unseen below the surface.

That is a lot that we don't see.

If we aren't careful, we can get our eyes so fixed on what is seen that we miss the unseen. When we get focused on stacking up things like cars, boats, houses, shoes, clothes, food, or... I don't know... comic books, or just about anything else, we have to be careful that greed doesn't grow in our hearts.

Greed tells us to get, while God tells us to give.

Jesus said that this "getting" thinking dominates unbelievers, but it doesn't have to be your story. There is a better way to live: seeking the Kingdom of God first, and trusting him to give you what you need. Sometimes, the Kingdom of God can be hard to see, especially, if you don't know what you are looking for. At a minimum it requires attentiveness, and maybe a few clues.

The Kingdom is seen in a hug to someone who feels unloved and lonely. The Kingdom is seen, when someone in a hurry, slows down to hold the door for someone else. The Kingdom is seen when the poor are fed, and the homeless are clothed. These things are often unseen and overlooked.

But, here is the truth: the more you look for the Kingdom, the more you will see the Kingdom. It may not be as obvious as cars, boats, houses, or whatever else you may think you need, but it is far more powerful!

What have you been seeking first?

How can you seek the Kingdom today?

Why do you worry about your needs?

Pray and ask God to give you an undivided heart that is loyal to him first and then the freedom to enjoy the good gifts he gives.

And I will give you a new heart, and I will put a new spirit in you. I will take out your stony, stubborn heart and give you a tender, responsive heart.

Ezekiel 36:26

DAY 77

May the words of my mouth and the meditation of my heart be pleasing to you, O Lord, my rock and my redeemer.

Psalm 19:14

Then Abraham looked up and saw a ram caught by its horns in a thicket. So he took the ram and sacrificed it as a burnt offering in place of his son.

Genesis 22:13

EXTRA TIME

Fulfillment

In this passage we find Abraham about to sacrifice his only son Isaac. Not because he wanted to, but because he was being obedient even to the point of death. It is at that moment when Abraham looks up and sees a ram caught in the thicket. At just the right time, God provides a substitute.

This story takes place on a mountain thousands of years before Jesus walked the face of this earth. People far smarter than I would tell you that Jesus was actually sacrificed on the cross during Passover at the 9th hour (3pm), at the same time as the traditional evening sacrifice, on the exact same mountain that God, so many years before, provided a substitute for Isaac.

It is because of Abraham's obedience that God promises to multiply his descendants like the stars of the sky, and promises that all the nations will be blessed because of them. In the Old Testament we see everything points ahead to Jesus. In the New Testament we see everything pointing back to Jesus.

Read Genesis 22 and note what points to Jesus, and any other things the Holy Spirit might be saying to you TODAY about obedience or listening for God's voice.

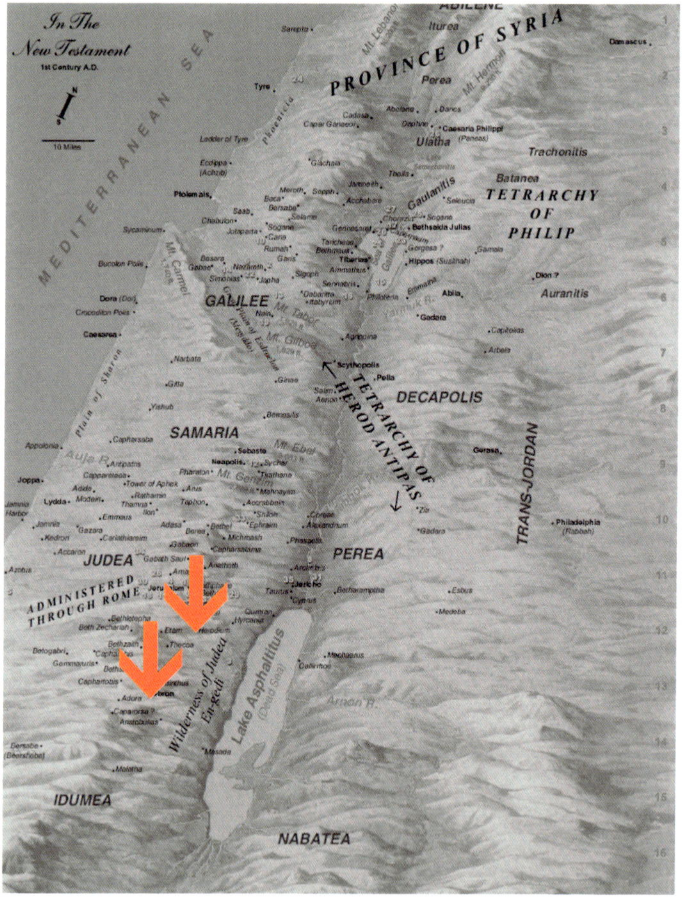
In The
New Testament
1st Century A.D.
10 Miles
MEDITERRANEAN SEA
PROVINCE OF SYRIA
Iturea
Perea
Damascus
Tyre
Ulatha
Trachonitis
Batanea
TETRARCHY
OF
PHILIP
Gaulanitis
Ptolemais
Bethsaida Julias
Hippos
Auranitis
GALILEE
Mt. Carmel
Mt. Tabor
Mt. Gilboa
Caesarea
Scythopolis
Pella
Gadara
DECAPOLIS
TETRARCHY OF
HEROD ANTIPAS
SAMARIA
Sebaste
Neapolis
Joppa
Lydda
Gerasa
TRANS-JORDAN
Philadelphia
(Rabbah)
JUDEA
ADMINISTERED
THROUGH ROME
PEREA
Jericho
Esbus
Medeba
Machaerus
Wilderness of Judea
En-gedi
Lake Asphaltitus
(Dead Sea)
Masada
IDUMEA
NABATEA

Sometime later, God tested Abraham's faith. "Abraham!" God called. "Yes," he replied. "Here I am." ²"Take your son, your only son—yes, Isaac, whom you love so much—and go to the land of Moriah. Go and sacrifice him as a burnt offering on one of the mountains, which I will show you." ³The next morning Abraham got up early. He saddled his donkey and took two of his servants with him, along with his son, Isaac. Then he chopped wood for a fire for a burnt offering and set out for the place God had told him about. ⁴On the third day of their journey, Abraham looked up and saw the place in the distance. ⁵"Stay here with the donkey," Abraham told the servants. "The boy and I will travel a little farther. We will worship there, and then we will come right back."⁶So Abraham placed the wood for the burnt offering on Isaac's shoulders, while he himself carried the fire and the knife. As the two of them walked on together,⁷Isaac turned to Abraham and said, "Father?" "Yes, my son?" Abraham replied. "We have the fire and the wood," the boy said, "but where is the sheep for the burnt offering?" ⁸"God will provide a sheep for the burnt offering, my son," Abraham answered. And they both walked on together. ⁹When they arrived at the place where God had told him to go, Abraham built an altar and arranged the wood on it. Then he tied his son, Isaac, and laid him on the altar on top of the wood.

¹⁰And Abraham picked up the knife to kill his son as a sacrifice. ¹¹At that moment the angel of the Lord called to him from heaven, "Abraham! Abraham!" "Yes," Abraham replied. "Here I am!" ¹²"Don't lay a hand on the boy!" the angel said. "Do not hurt him in any way, for now I know that you truly fear God. You have not withheld from me even your son, your only son." ¹³Then Abraham looked up and saw a ram caught by its horns in a thicket. So he took the ram and sacrificed it as a burnt offering in place of his son. ¹⁴Abraham named the place Yahweh-Yireh (which means "the Lord will provide"). To this day, people still use that name as a proverb: "On the mountain of the Lord it will be provided." ¹⁵Then the angel of the Lord called again to Abraham from heaven. ¹⁶"This is what the Lord says: Because you have obeyed me and have not withheld even your son, your only son, I swear by my own name that ¹⁷I will certainly bless you. I will multiply your descendants beyond number, like the stars in the sky and the sand on the seashore. Your descendants will conquer the cities of their enemies.¹⁸And through your descendants all the nations of the earth will be blessed—all because you have obeyed me."

Genesis 22:1-18

DAY 79

So we can say with confidence, "The Lord is my helper, so I will have no fear. What can mere people do to me?"

Hebrews 13:16

DAY 80

The one thing I ask of the Lord—the thing I seek most—is to live in the house of the Lord all the days of my life, delighting in the Lord's perfections and meditating in his Temple.

Psalm 27:4

⁵⁰Then Jesus shouted out again, and he released his spirit. ⁵¹At that moment the curtain in the sanctuary of the Temple was torn in two, from top to bottom. The earth shook, rocks split apart, ⁵²and tombs opened. The bodies of many godly men and women who had died were raised from the dead.

Matthew 27:50-52

EXTRA TIME

Structure

The temple had a large curtain separating the Holy of Holies from the other places of the temple. Historians estimate this curtain to be roughly 60 feet tall and four inches thick. That is one big curtain!

Once a year, the High Priest could enter into the Holy of Holies, the place where God's presence dwelt on Earth, and make atonement for the sins of the people. No one else was allowed to enter the Holy of Holies.

When Jesus gave up his spirit, the curtain was torn in two from top to bottom, something that would have been impossible for any human to accomplish. In this one moment Jesus' death dealt with sin once and for all, making it possible for sinful man to be near Holy God. Since the curtain was torn, God's presence was now readily available to all through Jesus Christ.

Those who believe in Jesus now become the temple of the Holy Spirit, reminding us that because Jesus is the Great High Priest, we now have access to God's Spirit all day, every day.

There is power in the name of Jesus! There was on that day, and there still is today.

Whatever situation you are facing today, know that God is powerful enough to handle it. Take a few minutes to be aware of the Holy Spirits' presence with you right now. Call upon his name. Cast your cares upon him. Rest in his presence knowing that He is near.

PS – In the passage, did you notice the walking dead that rose from the grave and made a cameo that day? Crazy!

DAY 82

And you must love the Lord your God with all your heart, all your soul, and all your strength.

Deuteronomy 6:5

DAY 83

Confess your sins to each other and pray for each other so that you may be healed. The earnest prayer of a righteous person has great power and produces wonderful results.

James 5:16

DAY 84

"How great you are, O Sovereign Lord! There is no one like you. We have never even heard of another God like you!"

2 Samuel 7:22

Journal

Take a few minutes to pour your heart out to God. Write what's on your mind, what's bothering you, ask him questions, and record what he has been speaking to you. Whatever it is, this space is for you.

DAY 85

"If you are faithful in little things, you will be faithful in large ones. But if you are dishonest in little things, you won't be honest with greater responsibilities."

Luke 16:10

DAY 86

[8] "My thoughts are nothing like your thoughts," says the Lord. "And my ways are far beyond anything you could imagine. [9] For just as the heavens are higher than the earth, so my ways are higher than your ways and my thoughts higher than your thoughts."

Isaiah 55:8-9

EXTRA TIME →

My Observations

Airplane Perspective.

Order v Chaos.

God is not surprised.

He is qualified.

Have you ever been in an airplane? What a different perspective than when we are walking on the Earth.

Down here things feel like chaos at times, but from an airplane everything looks like it is in order! From the airplane the roads are straight, the lights are all in line, the plots of land are all in squares, and the cars are all moving along nicely.

In the same way, God's ways and thoughts are coming from a different perspective. What looks like chaos in your life right now is only because of your limited perspective. The truth is, God is ordering your steps (Psalm 37:23).

Whatever you are facing today, He is not surprised by it. Surprised is one thing God has never been!

The good news is that whatever it is you are facing He is qualified to handle it.

Take a few minutes and cast your chaos on Him. Trust He sees your life from a much higher perspective.

DAY 87

The Lord isn't really being slow about his promise, as some people think. No, he is being patient for your sake. He does not want anyone to be destroyed, but wants everyone to repent.

2 Peter 3:9

So God created human beings in his own image. In the image of God he created them; male and female he created them.

Genesis 1:27

DAY 89

He took some bread and gave thanks to God for it. Then he broke it in pieces and gave it to the disciples, saying, "This is my body, which is given for you. Do this in remembrance of me."

Luke 22:19

EXTRA TIME →

Peace in Stillness

You have seen the famous Last Supper painting, right? That painting is a depiction of the historical event in Luke 22:19.

Jesus is sharing the Passover meal with his closest friends and he pours new meaning into some of the elements that are always at the table. In this particular verse, we see Jesus breaking the bread and identifying it as a symbol of his body which is about to be broken for them and for us on the cross.

There is an ancient Jewish tradition at the Passover meal in which the father breaks the bread and hides it around the table for the children. When the children find the bread they each receive a prize.

What's interesting in this passage is that Jesus doesn't hide the broken bread, in fact he does the opposite. He distributes the bread to all. Jesus' sacrifice on the cross, his broken body, is for all who would come to him.

It was once said that Christianity is the most inclusive and exclusive religion all at the same time. It is inclusive because the opportunity to place your faith in Jesus has been extended to all. All are welcome to enter into a relationship with God. It is also exclusive in that there is only way to do that. Jesus is the way, the truth, and the life. No one comes to the Father in Heaven except through Him (John 14:6).

One of the best ways for us to remember what Jesus has done for us is through communion. Believers are commanded to examine their hearts before receiving communion. It is a time to remember His sacrifice, reflect on its meaning, and repent of any sin in our hearts.

Take this time to practice communion on your own, or simply: remember, reflect, and repent. Know that wherever you are right now can be holy. You could be in a car, on a plane, at your house, in a hotel, or coffee shop. God desires to meet with you now in a tangible way. Pursue his presence.

When was the last time you slowed down to remember his body broken and blood shed for you? Take some time to listen for his voice and record what you hear.

DAY 90

Three things will last forever—faith, hope, and love—and the greatest of these is love.

1 Corinthians 13:13

What has God been teaching you over the last 90 days? How has he been speaking? Go back through all 90 days and record any major themes below.

How have you seen God answer your prayers? Go back through all 90 days and document his faithfulness here.

Conclusion

Close your scripture journal and look for the white box on the spine. Perhaps you have never noticed it, or perhaps you have been wondering what it's for.

The white box is for you to record the dates you worked through the scripture journal. It's a way to document this season of life and what God has been speaking to you during this time.

After recording the date, go ahead and put it on the shelf with your other books. In the months or years to come you will find yourself pulling out the scripture journal and remembering all that God said and all that God has done since that time.

In that moment you will find God to be more faithful than you ever knew.

Keep looking intently into his word and actively listening for his voice.

Notes